ISBN-13:9798563954700

Cover art and portraits by Blake Williams
Illustrations by Eli Brown

First U.S. edition. Printed in the United States of America

1

Contact Me:
Email: blakerwilliams@gmail.com
IG: @thatgreeneyedmixedguy

Acknowledgements

This book is a collection of stories, experiences, and people that I stitched together throughout my 20s. They were moments I never intended to share. I wrote them for myself as a means to survive.

As I got to the end of the writing process, I started to examine why I felt the need to take my secrets, my failures, my heartbreak, my trauma, and the most private moments of my life, and share them with the world.

I reflected on growing up as a gay black boy. How I never could find stories of lonely boys who felt like me falling in love with other lonely boys who felt like them.

So, I wrote my own.

The world needs more black stories. The world needs more gay stories. The world needs more stories about people who wake up every day and fight to survive mental illness.

This book exists so that perhaps someone who might not be used to reading stories about themselves may find their place in this complicated world. A place where they matter.

For all the ones who said I love you and meant it, I love you too. So much. You are worth more than I would get if I sold all the stars I've ever wished on back to the galaxy.

If you're reading this, and you feel lost... you're not. You just haven't gotten there yet.

If you're reading this, thank you.

These stories mean everything to me.

We Were Young Until Young Until We Were Broken
very short stories about very long nights

Lived By: Blake Williams

Table of Contents

7

~~mAnIC~~
Part I

BiPolar

I would do so many things differently if I could.
But I wouldn't change a thing.

—

9

Summer 2015 | Auburn

The night my spine faded into a whisper,
you came outside and found me
underneath those small-town stars.
You laid down next to me.
Instead of talking, we stared at the stars like
they were miracles that finally came true.

The Best I Could Do With Who I Was At The Time

These poems were supposed to be tombstones where everyone I've ever let go of could spend eternity, hidden inside metaphors and apologies.

Please, when you're learning how to forgive me, know my life was never as easy as it was broken.

My love was never as guarded as my secrets.

My mouth has its own heart, that beats like the stars and starting over.
And over.
And over.

I was always so good at the beginning.

CHAOS

I spent so much time

Dancing through fire

When I finally

Found

Peace. I didn't know if I should stayor
L   E   A   V   E

Have you ever felt
Like the only way to get the voices in your head
To be quiet is to

SCREAM
LOUDER

I'M SO COMFORTABLE IN

CHAOS

Imstartingtowonderifilikewakingupfeelingbroken

13

Tiny

I want everyone to know,
You saved my life that summer.
I'll never understand how all your broken parts
were strong enough to hold on to mine.

I
    Was
            Falling
                    So
                          Fast.

Percocet

So many people say they have no regrets.
I can't say I feel the same way.
There are so many nights where
I can't sleep because of all the damage I've done.

Boys Don't Cry
(Body Armor)

Every day, I will try to smile the paint back
into all the sunrises you raped from me.

Sorry Mama

The last time I saw my parents,
I smiled through dozens of lies.

I didn't want them to notice just how much the light had
faded from my eyes.

I'm so tired of breaking my Mother's heart.

W I N O N A (fucking) B L V D.

You might come to find
That when you left me in the dark,
My whole world fell apart
I stood there waiting.

Hoping you would run back in and
Maybe try to save me from the part
Where you left me out there, waiting.

HOLLYWOOD

These streets are for getting lost in.

f u c k. y o u.

if i should see you anytime soon
i would strip the sunday light from your eyes
i'd pinprick the beauty from your conditioned smile
and bitch slap the façade off your tongue.
you left me as empty as the words that lay the foundation
to all the promises you ever broke.

Boycrush

We could have been once in a lifetime.

Rain on a tin roof.

As dumb as we were happy.

Infinitely nostalgic.

Like every song was ours.

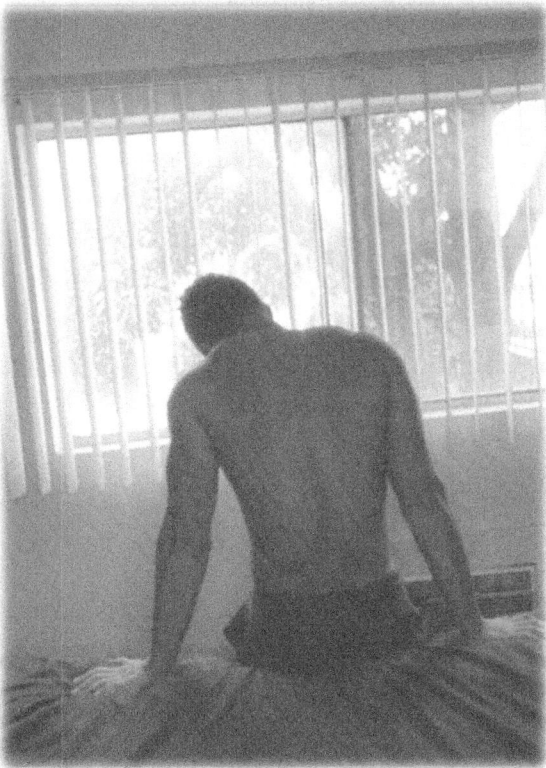

Just A Small Town Boy

She said she doesn't trust me anymore.
Says things are different and her guard is up,
I said *when did my love become something you had to be afraid of?*

It holds you the same.

Sometimes, the people you love most in the world don't
remember the wars you fought together on your way down to
rock bottom.

We
                Landed
                                Together.

We broke at the same seam. I helped you rebuild, and you
walked me away from that ledge.

You held me, and said *I'll be your home.*

I captured all your wasted breaths and gave them back to you
with the best nights of our lives.

We watched so many sunrises.
We laughed through so many nights.

That balcony was home to all the orphan in me.

Your couch kept me out of my car.
Your food kept me full.
Our talks kept me alive.

Your voice, was like the sweetest hit,

Baby, I would have
        Faded
            For
                You.

Disappeared from this life and waited for you in the next. I. Fell. So. Hard.

I know we're all made in the image of a God, and just like god, humans never seem to show up when they're supposed to.

I was so sick, of this life and that empty apartment. I got too comfortable with those empty bottled white line lies.

I was just trying to forget what it feels like to be forgotten.

So, kiss me, like a broken hallelujah. Send me on my way. Pretend we never filled each other's hearts. Forget the love.

Forget the stories.

Forget the secrets.

But I'm begging you not to forget me.

Take me with you.

Or at least, come back for the pieces.

Where'd You Go?

What happened to that boy?
The one who wasn't afraid to love
Like he had nothing to lose.

Sisters Save Lives
(for Poosin)

You were always braver than me.
Tougher too, but somehow, just as soft.
If you hadn't drawn first blood,
I'd still be running from all the things I knew to be true.
I'd be screaming at the gates of heaven.
Begging God to find room in his omnipotent heart,
for all the love I could never find for myself.
You showed me how bright we are
when we finally stop hiding in the dark.

"straight" boy

Do you remember when you said my laugh sounded like the living room of an unbroken family on Christmas morning, and I told you, your arms were like towers?

I swear I won't tell how you leaned in to kiss me and tried to make it look like an accident. We left so much unsaid.

I was always the first person you'd call and the only one you'd stay up to watch the sunrise with. How many stars did we launch off that balcony hoping that at least one dream might come true? We held onto them the same way we held on to each other through the hardest parts of that entire year.

I still don't know how you paid for that apartment on Wilshire when we never had enough money for a full stomach.

I'll never understand how you were so easy to talk to. I just know we couldn't get enough of each other.

What would have happened, if we touched the truth the way our hands touched the scars left over from all the things our parents couldn't protect us from?

What would we have found if we had stayed? What would we have found, if you weren't so afraid of someone finding all the tears you keep hidden behind those towers?

I know you loved how it felt to touch me.

Did you think I didn't already know how far you were from home? Didn't you see I was trying to build you a new one?

College
I made love to as many of those
dance floors as I could go home with.

Ms. Paige

Your face plays like my favorite broken record through every childhood summer.

Memories of dancing on an old carpet in an even older mobile home until every part of our bodies was sore. Laying on the deck of boat near the lake on the warmest midnights of our youth.

Talking until the sun came up. Laughing until our faces hurt and our cheeks burned with the most naïve of tears.

We would sit on the porch while all the older kids watched "R" rated movies with our parents.

We'd talk about God, and how confusing it was to love him.

We loved each other like our souls were made to love like soulmates. You were always easy.

We never talked about boys, and we stopped talking when I told the world I loved one.

There are days I wonder how you're still not here.

How you live knowing you never called me back.

5 years later, and I still don't understand how you walked away, and made it look so fucking easy.

mentiroso

In the end, you used me
Like a napkin that was too small to wipe off
The heartbreak written across my face.
I bet I tasted so good.

Trauma always does.

We Will End

Left with all the holes we dug into each other's hearts trying
to make room for all the parts god spent eternity forgetting.

La Carcel

I'm so sorry I stopped showing up.
It's a sin I don't think deserves forgiveness.
You would never have left me like that.
Everything in your life was falling apart.
Everyone you loved had left.
I know how dark it gets in those woods when you're out there
alone at night.
I'm so sorry.
I'm so sorry.
I'm so sorry.
Thank you, for taking me back.
I swear, I'll never leave you like that again.
I will never let you look alone for light in a world this dark.

Church Kid

The joy slipped out of my eyes
the way smoke prays its way
out of the end of those blunts.
The ones we built our home with when god stopped
answering our prayers.

There were whole years where the only altar I worshiped
was the last call of an empty bar
and 6 am pillow talk with strangers.
Nothing else felt safe.
Nowhere else felt holy.
We may have been lost, but we still had another bottle
and a little more time.

We were just kids on drugs.
Waking up on balconies, in love.
It was a summer, in our 20s,
you were perfect, and I was happy.

We made a sanctuary out of our secrets.

I keep yours, tucked in between all the things
I'm still afraid of.

B.A.W. III

You were the first person who made me feel like
I could risk everything.

Your name is stitched into the lining of the fabric
on everything I do.

p. a. t. h. e. t. i. c.

Am I a fool to think I could wake up one day as more than a
tragedy and not feel like I stole from you?

Smoke and Mirrors

Cigarettes come 20 in a pack each time.
I know what to expect each time.
Wish I could say the same about, friends of mine.

We got high...
Maybe I pushed them all away.
Still no one, ever called to say, are you okay?

Pour me another drink.
I might really have a problem.
Maybe another line will solve them.
No one, no one's calling me...

I know, that this is a familiar story.
It's not uncharted territory,
But my bottle is far from empty.

There's really not a way to say this.
Some days the pain and loss feel endless.
I swear I'll take this up with God.
He knows I've got some questions for him.
Like, *Jesus, what about those orphans?*

I got so lost in smoke.
I'm so afraid of mirrors.
I told my Mama, nothing to see here.

I'm just a ghost.

It's been three months since I've been sober.
I thought my life was finally over.
I'm on the edge...

Pull me out of my grave.

COCAINE

I laughed harder than I cried.

MANIC

I remember the night the stars fell out of the middle of the sky and landed on the tips of my fingers. We drove alongside the beach with the windows rolled down and the music as loud as those '92 Corolla speakers could go.

I locked my hands together and prayed a galaxy out of my dreams. You loved me so well.

I never smiled as brightly.
It spilled out of my mouth like a Scripture at the end of a shameless sinner's first one-night stand.

We ran through the parts of the city the streetlights forgot about.

All I remember is the taste of red wine and the sound of my laugh. The way it danced off the walls of downtown like we were teenagers, in love, swinging over a lake in the middle of the summer.

You made so much sense of my madness.
For the first time I wasn't crazy, I was brilliant.

My mind was a Monument of Dreams.
I was so afraid I would lose you.

With you, every moment felt like getting high for the first time. The world wrapped itself around me the way you wrap yourself around the people you no longer have to lie to.

I lived for years with a heart that was never anything but damaged, but with you, I was a thousand perfect nights. It was nothing but love and lights. There were so many people around me all holding on to the edge of their lives with the one or two dreams that they still hadn't lost.

We'd stay up all night. Writing poems in between the white lines of our most private notebooks.

I gave everything I had to people who won't remember my name. I was always the last one awake.

I would roam the streets with no place to go but my secrets. Some nights, I go to sleep so afraid of who I might be in the morning. I never know who I'm going to be in the morning.

I never know how much I'm going to lose until I finally land back inside this body.

I always have to write so many *I'm sorrys.*

The morning always comes, and with it, all the human in me. You always made me feel more beautiful than I was, and I always caught you lying when the sun came in through that window on Winona.

I'll never forget the way we would scrape together just enough for one last blunt, and one last omelet, using food stolen off the plates of the richest and most famous people in the world.

We'd listen to BLONDE on repeat and talk about all the boys we ever loved.

We were young until we were broken.

And I was happy, until I saw how faraway I was from the person I kept pretending to be.

And from you.

The one who kept me from falling apart and always helped me pick up the pieces from all the things I'd fucked up the night before.

I was so tired.

I was so sick.

I was so close to writing the saddest ending to the most beautiful song.

Will you please come back?

Don't forget your promise to bring me the stars.

I'll wait for you, here in the dark.

Calligraphy of Fallen Stars
Part 2

I swear, I'm less poetic in person.

Dance | Break

Dancing in the dirt like it was the gold paved streets of
heaven, they moved like the world was watching,
but they didn't notice.

Dreaming like they had forgotten how to wake up.

Laughing, like it would put food on the table.

The Lost Boys

We're like sand.
You can't find the parts that fit together.

Like rain falling from the same cloud,
we look nothing like we used to.

So, we'll just lie here in pieces,
separated in all the most important places.

Ometepe

I know you remember the night we laughed over
plantains and dozens of Smirnoff Ice.

We sat stunned by the volcanos and the waterfalls.
We kept asking each other
how we were living these incredible lives.
For once everything was going right.

We drove motorcycles around that entire island until we
cried falling asleep on the 2nd story balcony of an
abandoned building overlooking the ocean.

The rain fell that night and we talked about all the people
who had broken our hearts.

I'll always remember how much love existed between us.
It was like nothing could tear us a part.
Not even time or lies.
There are some people you just trust with your life.

Unlike God, she left me better than she found me.

Te Prometo
(Nini)

I'll hold onto you.
Until the world ends.

Desamparados

I'll always remember the way the rain sounded
outside your bedroom window.
The home of Maria's voice as it danced through that kitchen,
healing all of us.
I think about the picture of the little girl laughing
in the ocean for the first time.
I think about that boy, the one I kept falling in love with,
but could never keep safe.
I remember how the anger turned to ice,
and we forgot who the fuck we were.
I know we cried through so many of those mornings,
knowing our tears could never save any of those kids
no matter how many of them we let
break through the prayers in our eyes.
I know God never showed up.
I know how many battles we've survived.
I know time doesn't make the memories any easier.
I know our tears don't make their lives any better.
I know how many times your heart stopped.
I know how much it hurt you to leave.
I'll protect our stories for the rest of my life.
I tattooed their names on my arm because
you know I just couldn't let them go.
I think about Desmparados, every day.
I know you do too.

Calligraphy of Fallen Stars

I'm so sorry, for all the things I couldn't love you free from.
For watching the light fade from your eyes like a wilted
summer. The way we left our love, nothing more or less than
an unkept promise, the dungeons of doubt imprisoned our
abandoned souls. We couldn't even feel God.

I'm so over these empty midnights. Even the stars look
fractured. Even the moon looks tired.

I grieved your death until I cradled my own. I've sung
orphans to sleep and then in the same day spent $100
on dinner.

I've tried to shove the pain into as many one nights stands as
I could find empty nights for, but there's nothing healing
about losing yourself inside of a stranger's pain.

I remember the night I told my best friend, that even while
he called the street corner his home, that God was still good.
If that was love, then crucify my obituary and paint brush the
pages with my blood-stained tears, I'm torn in half.

So, make me a light house, so everyone I've ever loved can
find their way home, no matter how ugly the storm.

I remember falling into dust, when our loved ached like the
sunset bruised with loss, and we stood, bare. And all we had
left was hope in a god we still hadn't met like there was still
something missing, like a city void of lost boys. There was an
afterglow of all those stories living along the same shore. Fill
my laugh lines with broken concrete and a good smoke.

Remember when forever fell into the flames of a fire we lost
our hands in.

I miss your touch. It's the same way God must have missed his son, but what good is heaven, if everyone you've ever loved is on fire?

So tonight, I wanna burn.
Tonight, I wanna wash over those faded memories.

I'm reaching with arms wide open hoping to graze the infinity of your soul, but as I stared around at this broken planet, I couldn't shed a single virtuous tear.

I'm gonna to the let the sky break for me into a Calligraphy of Fallen Stars...

Thank God for the music.

Thank God for tonight.

That God for everyone who ever said *I LOVE YOU* and meant it.

The ones that kept me alive on those nights when every breath was like a broken monument waiting to be held, and every heart, beat like a broken prayer.

Eclipse my wounds.

Plant a garden in the bed of my sin so even my ruin is lined with petals.

I'm at the end of every rope I've ever tried to tie around my promises, so my God, love me back to the light I was born out of.

I was never meant to stay lost for so long, so give me a second chance.

Forgive my damage. Love the hate out of my fear.

I think I'm finally ready to hold on again, and this time... maybe the letting go won't tear me apart.

I can't go out like that.

I wanna love, like this life ripped me apart, but hope... never let me go.

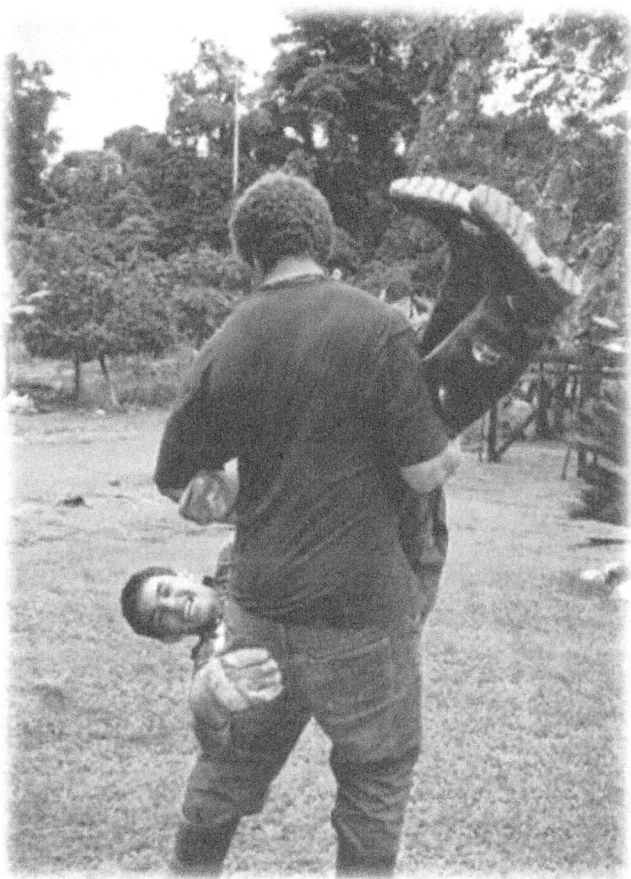

The Night of My 21st Birthday

The legs of the city were lined with 13-year-old girls who
knew way too much about their bodies, and not enough
about their souls.

They understood the phrase *how much* in 12 different
languages but couldn't produce any eloquent soliloquies
in their own.

The leftover downtown lights paraded them around at
midnight like hand-picked stars.

All the right curves on all the too young faces.
Smiles that had no truth to their creases.
Couldn't even light up the painted glitter spread like a
knee to the asphalt across their faces.

Their legs were smooth like moonlight river nights
crescendo-ing into fucked up twilights, crowned with
Tower of Babylon heels, that reverberated off the walls
of a city god had all but forgotten, like an 80s bass line
beating down the throats of tourists like an acidic fog.

I learned the hard way, that there will always be children
forced to use their bodies as a sacrifice to survive the
men in this world.

They will laugh trying to hide the corpse we made of
their youth.

You can't hide pain under mascara.
You can't mask sadness under foundation.

The crack from that break is too broken for crosses.

I'll never forget what it felt like, to see someone completely lost and completely alone in a world full of people who forgot they were children.

And then I got on a bus to go celebrate all the freedom I was born into.

What a fucking privilege to wake up every day and be able to pretend the world isn't being set on fire.

Sometimes, I wonder how God looks himself in the mirror.

Growing up Christian

God sent his son to earth to die on a cross.

Why the fuck did we ever think he'd give a shit
about us?

Leave. Me. Alone.

I never meant to love anyone like that.
I hope I can figure out how to fall asleep and wake
up without you always being the last and first thing on
my mind. . .

Even my tears know when thoughts of you are on
their way... they hide.

Usually in time.

Alajuelita

I finally understand why you respected those streets
like they were the father you never had.

fuck

They were right… you can't fix people.

Sandpaper

Promise me this… when the trumpets fade, you'll
remember when I loved goosebumps down your spine.

Promise me you won't fade away, like the last notes of
a symphony.

Promise me you'll remember the night when we named
all the stars we could see, before their light faded.

Don't you dare fade on me.

I loved you, in every way I could think of, but none of
the ways you needed

I keep wishing that my hands were made of sandpaper,
so the things that matter would

       stop

          slipping

              through.

Ben Howard and Sweet Potato Fries

I remember the day you became a mom. I drove 3 hours in traffic because you said if I didn't, you'd be alone. You said he wasn't coming. No one was coming. So, we stood on that pier and cried like the world was ending. You held me, like I was the only thing that could keep your lungs from screaming their way out of your chest.

Only you and I know about those rooftops in Haiti, and the faith we lost on that tour bus.

You gave me so many reasons to stay.

Do you remember the night I finally told the truth? I stopped sleeping on the floor and crawled into your bed. We turned on Strivers Row, put that shit on repeat, and I learned the easiest way to be nothing but honest, was behind a mic, on a stage, with you in the front row catching all of my tears.

We always hugged harder than we kissed.
I never touched you like I wanted you.
It was always like I loved you.

I remember all the poems we cried in pubs over burgers and sweet potato fries. Our laughs, ruining everyone else's dinner. We'd drink until everything didn't hurt like hell.

Our hearts always beat like war drums. Our eyes pointed to the sky as the sun set over the ocean screaming about how mortal infinity felt.

It was all those broken stilettos and cracked falsettos. How we always found the most broken girls crying on curbs outside of bars. They were always alone, always like a mirror.

We were just chaos and sunsets.

Screaming out the windows of your Honda, from Huntington to Manila, we found love in so many Armageddon hearts.

Love was holding each other when the rest of the world couldn't find room for all the fires we set. We took long drives to nowhere and spent even longer nights looking for empty pubs where we could leave all the saddest stories we carried. The ones we hid behind all the bones the world kept breaking.

We faded into the sin stained on the holes of so many dance floors. Like if we could sweat out all the fragments left over from all the people we had lost, maybe it would finally start raining.

I asked God to make me a lighthouse.

I sang songs about girls I never really loved and boys I hadn't yet met. I thought you found me at rock bottom. I thought I saved you from yours.

You kept falling in love with men who only knew how to hurt you, and that's how I found you.

And you found me, with ashy elbows, endlessly misunderstood, with a heart like a mountain nobody could climb.

I still think about you and Bobby.

I still wonder why you never showed up in West Hollywood, like you swore you would.

That night, I left all the poems I had ever written you on a curb outside of a gay bar full of everyone I loved. Except you. I hoped that some drunk girl with a broken heart, fake hair, and 6-inch stilettos might find them. Maybe even on one of the saddest nights of her life, the way I so often found you.

Maybe she could finally figure out what to do with all the poems we wrote about all the people we survived.

I hope she loves them as much as you did.

ALL THE THINGS WE LOST ALONG THE WAY
Part 3

Baby don't you worry.
We're gonna be just fine.
We're gonna be alright.
I know we can make it
But we gotta stay and fight.
I'll fight all night.

P U L S E: For Marsha P Johnson

Is there no safe place, for us?
They burned our homes.
Shot our brothers.
Took the best of us...
Ripped us from their pages.
Said we weren't here.
But I'm still here.
And damnit, you're still here.

Let's remind them.
Our love is deeper.
Because it's rooted,
In all we lost.

You can't erase us.
We're not invisible.
We're far from finished
So far from over.
No, we won't forget.
The ones you stole from us.
You stole so much from us.

George Floyd

I woke up to a world on fire.
Our cities shattered like a chandelier of hate.
An orchard of ruined mothers and angry brothers.
All our hearts broke at the same time.

They called our tears riots.

Primetime

Hell only makes the news when it's
burning the streets where white kids play

blackaf

I keep waking up to black kids getting shot by cops.
I wonder if God has trouble hearing our prayers.
Maybe that's why he made our tears so god damn loud.
There are entire nights I can't sleep.
When all I hear is the sound of Black Mothers.

Screaming.

Black Magic

Where I come from,
People get scared when they see a nigga in a durag.

To them, we were never Kings protecting crowns

NIGHTMARE

The last thing I remember is always the same.
It's a little boy with my face and my heart.
He's crying.
He's always crying.
He asks me,
Why do they want to kill us?
I never have an answer.

BOYS

Part 4

Save me, from a lonely grave
Remind me what it hurt like
To love like an explosion of lights.

Drama Queen

Don't tell me to stop hurting.
God left me so lonely.
Even midnight has the stars.

I always hated when you'd call me dramatic.
Like somehow it hurt me less,
Cause I'm not afraid to show it.

If we could go back,
I would go back and change a couple things.
Cause this just doesn't feel right to me.

It's not like I left and just forgot about it.
I just didn't know that you cared enough to fix it.

And the worst thing, about it,
Is the way my heart heard it.
Cause that's not how you felt about me.

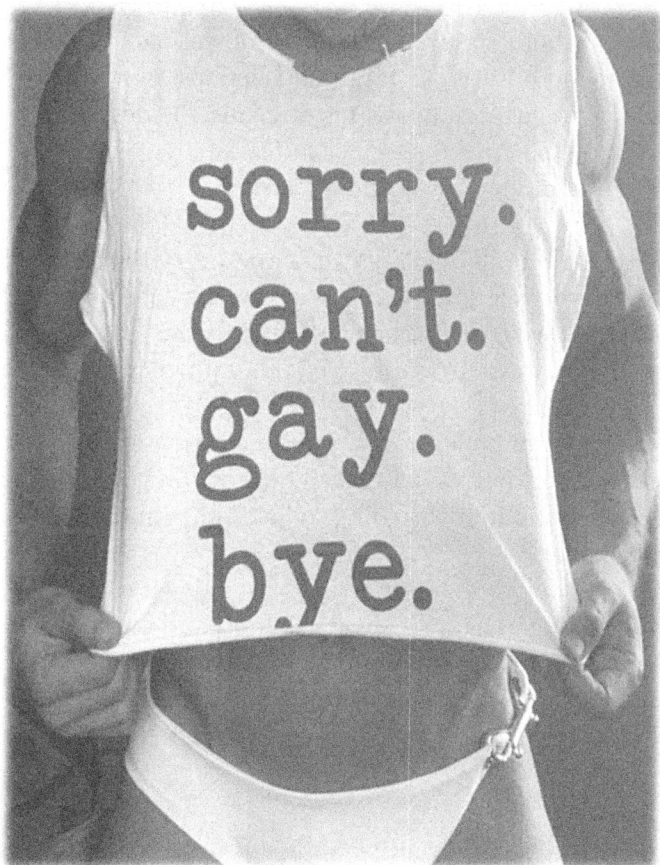

Joshua Tree

I knew you loved me, when you wouldn't stop reaching for my hand in the darkness until you finally found it.

I knew there wasn't a single place I wanted to be more than where I was. Everything I had lost was waiting for me in the arms of a boy, his dog, and the desert.

We laid in that hot spring for hours.

We laughed till our faces hurt, and everything I loved about you fell down the side of my face while Rufus Du Sol took us to the other side of the world, and then back to that empty yard in the middle of nowhere.

Do you remember how bright that moon was? Do you remember how we fell asleep outside, underneath a blanket of infinity listening to love songs and telling each other stories?

Like why my heart is always so loud and broken, and why you matter so much to me. I know you have no idea what to do with my stories. Neither do I, and neither does God, but I hope you understand why I feel so much.

I stayed awake and listened to you sleep as I wrote the most important poem of my life, and when the sun finally came up, I knew I would love you for the rest of mine.

If you ever walk away, I would never blame you. But I would always miss you.

You know I will always (always), leave the light on.

The Night Nobody Could Tell Us We Were Wrong

During the day, the high-rise buildings sit upon cracked concrete foundations like a good omen. The busy streets move like liquid falling though hands aged by hard work and prejudice. The streets twist like lies, lined with all the stains left by time and one-night stands.

Culture fills your nose; hummus, hot pan dulce, tandoori chicken, carne asada, the most delicious pineapple you've ever tasted…

The food is always better off the street, made by people taught by mothers who cook to heal.

Lovers hold hands under pea coats and coffee cups, stealing kisses behind centuries of history.

There is nothing like seeing a young person walk through a city for the first time. Like a newborn horse with wiry legs, and unbridled ambition.

I watched as the city romanced my 16-year-old brother out of adolescence. I watched him fall in love with strangers, foreign languages, the streets filled with talent, and the unyielding smell of marijuana.

I watched as he lifted is face to the sky on 9th, took a deep breath and laughed *you belong to me.*

These cities keep breaking my heart. Like when I tripped and got lost in a warehouse with my best friend, a drug dealer, and a prostitute. I spent the whole night, doing lines off the hands of strangers like I knew it was my last dance.

I remember the moment I saw him like a dream from across the dancefloor. We couldn't take our eyes off each other. Too high to be scared, I walked over and pressed my mouth up against his, and I swear to God as soon as I did, my favorite song came on.

We smoked blunts and laughed. We took pictures and hid in bathroom stalls. We disappeared outside, and I kissed you up against a fence until 5 in the morning. You were the boy I always wanted to meet afterhours, high, in a warehouse hiding in LA.

We danced until the police showed up.
We kissed as the sun came up.
Two brown boys, in love.
Not with each other but with that night.

Just like that boy, the city stays a mystery.
I keep falling in and out of love.

It's the oceans, the skylines, the late nights, and the people who make you feel like fiction.

It's the parties full of drugs you've never heard of and people you'll never remember. It's the friends who find you and then leave you fractured.

It's the fame and fear. It's feeling lonely in a city of 4 million people

It's the rooftop gardens and the fire escapes. It's surviving on a couple of dollars and a handful of dreams.

The teenage love and the street tacos. It's dancing with thousands of strangers in an empty field as the sun sets, and getting lost inside bars with terrible music and the last of your money. It's kissing pretty boys in bathroom stalls where nobody could tell us we were wrong.

The beauty of the city is captured in the heart of those who fall in love with the hedonistic arch in her spine and the artistic conviction of her mind. The hope that anyone can become anything.

I keep going back looking for that boy from the warehouse. I just want to know what falling in love feels like. I never found him. Or that high. Even though, for years, I tried.

Green Eyed Mixed Guy

He keeps talking about my eyes.
Some men think your ego is more
vulnerable than your heart.

He keeps answering questions I never ask
while ignoring the ones that I do.

I think he wants me to like him.

He keeps talking about my eyes,
like that's the most interesting thing about me.

I've met so many gay boys masquerading as men
still trying to fit into their father's clothes.
They'll tell you all about their job, but nothing about
the ghosts they keep tied around their ankles.

They'll spend all night telling you you're beautiful, never ask
what makes your heart break, and then wonder why you're
not more interested in how much they want you.

He keeps talking about my eyes. He asks me if I got them
from my Mom or my Dad.   I tell him I'm adopted.
He thinks he smells daddy issues on my tears
so he asks if I want another drink.

I ask for a double, even though
I promised myself I'd stop drinking.

He keeps talking about my eyes.

72

sexting(me)

I spent last night wide awake praying you weren't copying or pasting our conversations into the whispers of another boy's late-night pillow talk.

scared shitless

We are distant, and I'm worried, because I love you. From the bottom of my complicated heart...
I love you.

gay

So many people have broken my heart.
Haven't I lost enough?

life hack

I kept trying to explain myself.
I could never just shut the fuck up and listen.

the cycle

Him: I'm doing my fucking best.

Me: I know.

Hindsight: We both were.

Bad Habit

I'm probably better off with you.
I can't believe I really mean that.

This could be a huge mistake.
But babe, I've to walk away.

We tried and tried, but it's not working.
No one but ourselves to blame.

I won't let you try to fool me.
It happens when you say my name.

Babe... please don't say my name.

Minneapolis, Minnesota

He smelled like blunts.
He sounded like an unbroken smile.
I held him like he was the last moment of my life.
I loved him like he was the only promise God ever kept.

The Boulevard

I was 23 when I fell in love with Hollywood.
I was on stage in an acting class, the entire room
disappeared, and for the first time I found a safe place to
put all the feelings that never fit inside my body.

But just like that first boy, it didn't matter how tightly I
held onto him, we were never going to make it.

Sometimes, I feel like I'm the last person on earth who is
still awake. I've spent so many nights high and alone,
3am feels like a second home. A place I go when I'm too
poor to get out of the city.

We all talk about how lonely it is, but then we hide
behind so many walls, and excuses, and dreams, and
hustles, and bodies, and drugs, and parties.

What does it all matter, if as soon as we get back to these
empty apartments none of us can afford, we all fall apart
and start wondering, *is there's enough heaven left on earth
to stay?*

So many of us just want to be touched without having to
take our clothes off. We keep looking for God at the
rock bottom of people whose names we never knew.

I think the moon knows all my secrets. The only time I
ever told the whole truth was tripping down Hollywood
Blvd. on one of the saddest nights of my life. I was about
to let go of everything.

I remember when the only thing keeping me alive was
the sound of Jamie's laugh, that boy, that balcony where
he kissed me, and those $2 honey flavored white owls.

I remember losing God to a kid in Costa Rica who I'll never stop thinking about, and then found him in the arms of a drug addict at the end of a one-night stand in Las Vegas.

I've used so many bodies trying to find a way to feel comfortable in my own.

I'm always surprised by how dark it can really get when we all start telling the truth.

I would spend weeks dancing in piles of drunk snow laughing with strangers who told me everything they swore would stay secret.

For one night, none of us were alone.

I don't know what to do with all of these stories. But I'll keep the ones where my heart broke into the most pieces.

I love this city, like all the promises I've ever kept. I forgave myself for all the things I did to survive when I felt like I didn't matter and got lost in all the lights.

There were so many nights I thought would be the last. Like when I thought he was in love, when the whole time, I was just his fucking drug.

I fell completely apart.

I was so tired of holding on to this shipwrecked heart. So, I poured another glass, did a couple more lines, and lit one last Nat Sherman.

—

I walked under the moon, and as soon as I was ready to leave…

she asked me for another secret.

last call in Vegas

I don't know what that was.
We were never together.
So why did it feel like we were over?

I had to call and say goodbye.
I'm so glad you answered, but I'm so sorry I left you like an unfinished chapter.

I know we never said it, but I love you.
I think you know that.

I hung up and cried.

It was the first time since that night when you told me nobody looked at you the way I did.

You said you loved how excited I get when I talk about the things I feel matter.

You said I made you fall in love with people you'd never met. We both had a thing for beautiful people. The kind that hold your empty body while your soul finds its way back from wherever we go when we're gone.

We fell asleep to Jhene Aiko and like every time before, I left. Before the sun woke you up.

Bubba

We kept forgetting, the only thing we promised was that we'd try our best.

I should have just made space for you to be less than the man I dreamed of. We are never the people we dream about.

We are human, not ghosts, or gods.

We are distant, and I'm worried, but I'll leave my heart as open as my arms.

Tell me why we're standing here, in the same kitchen we fell in love in, talking about spending the next part of our lives without holding each other's hand.

I lost sleep, and you lost your mind.
We laughed, and God knows we cried, but it wasn't always sad. It wasn't even mostly sad.

It was epic, it was brilliant.
We were like a first dance to a song with no ending.

Every smile in every photo was real.

How did we break all the love we built in that apartment?

Like the virus had won. Like we were done.

Baby, I want you... forever.

They say every good thing comes to an end. Don't let go of my hand so we can prove them wrong.

You are the one thing I told God to promise he wouldn't take from me.

The only man I want.

When I think about a world without you...

Everything goes dark.

Pieces

Before you break my heart,
Before we both give up,
Can I just say this?

I don't know where this is going.
We're both still learning.
I know I'm learning.

But if I fall,
Will you pick me up and help me stand?
Promise me you'll be there,
If I break into pieces.
You know I need this.
Sometimes it feels a little like you're leaving.
Like you won't miss me.

I don't think that this is how it's supposed to feel.
I keep leaving you hurting.
Our house is burning.

you fucked me uuuuuuuuup

You taught me the value of building walls.
It'll be awhile before I let someone pickpocket my mind,
looking to steal my dreams.

Idiots

Look at our hands.
Just callouses and scars.
The only thing we did right,
was break each other's hearts.
Voices raised like cowards...
Why did we stop writing each other love notes?
It was the cheapest way to say, "I love you."

Manhattan

The last time I was in New York City, I fell in love.
I was walking alone from the Empire State Building to
the Brooklyn Bridge.

I spent the entire time pretending his hand was in mine.
I know it's weird, but I talked out loud as if he was there.
Up until that moment it was the closest to being in love I
was ever allowed to be.

I smiled the entire night and lived out every teenage
fantasy, like for once I didn't have so many things to
hide.

It was the most romantic night of my life.
I was so close to being me, I didn't care that I was alone,
walking through New York City at 2 in the morning.

I had no idea where to go.

No one was answering their phones.
No one invited me out.

I should have been sad, but I was in New York, and I
was in love with a boy. I have so many secrets.

Like the three way I had with coupled strangers when I
finally got back to my room.

They were so kind.

So excited.

So, in love.

With each other and that moment.

It was almost like I was even there, and I loved that. This was for them, and I wanted to give them that. I wanted them to love New York City as much as I did.

I knew then, that forever looks different for everybody.

They looked just as deeply into each other's eyes.

If anything, something about it felt safer.

GROWING PAINS

She gave up crying when she learned
that tears aren't strong enough to hold you.
Neither are men.
Neither are women.
She loved them both past trusting.
It's a mistake she's still too young to recover from.
There is so much more to life than running back to a
home you'll lose yourself never finding.

Friend With Benefits

That awkward moment when you're starting to fall in
love, and then you realize… to him, you're just a really
(and I mean, *really*) good fuck…

Cool.

Hurry Up, We're Dreaming

I moved the chair over to the windowsill.

I lit a cigarette and I watched the clouds form cities above rooftops and trees.

I could feel everything.

I thought about how winter gossips down the spine of fall. Whispering secrets like grey clouds over tin roofs.

I wonder what you thought about November, or If you still think about that first time. When hands were for holding, and naps were things you never did alone.

I hate falling asleep alone.

Sometimes I wake up from a dream and it feels like God left us here without a way out. There are mornings that are so human I can't trust my knees to take me to an honest prayer.

Don't let history books forget how we held hands and carried loved ones out of graveyards and on to thrones.

Don't let them forget how some of us stood strong, ankle deep in heartache, and waist deep in prejudice.

Tomorrow is just a few secrets away, so love me like my heart is a casket where your fears can go to die.

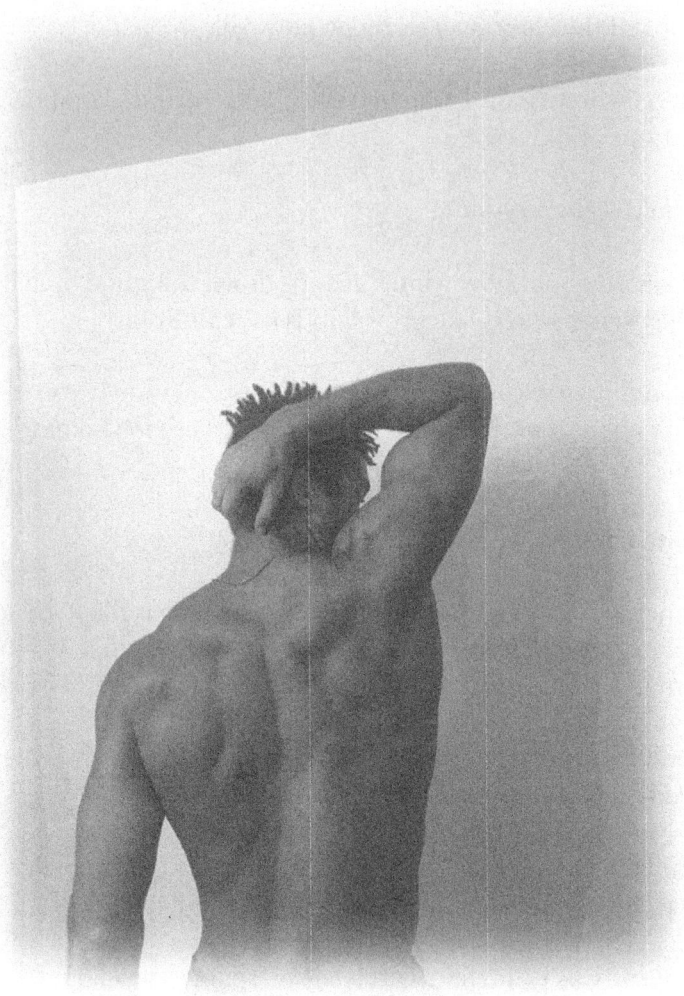

Insomniac

if i could find a way to make my laugh heal the pain caused
by losing loved ones i would bottle it up and i would make
joke after joke after joke so this bitterness inside my mouth,
on my tongue and all around my insides would stop
suffocating the hope and joy out of me. wouldn't stab my
peace in the back and leave it out to die if i could pluck the
stars from space, hold them in my palms, close my eyes, and
count to ten, then throwthem back up at the sky without
watching where they would land,just to say i had a hand in
the way the universe was formed i would then ask, whoever
put them there in the first place, why he kept them so far
away from us and do shooting stars really make our dreams
come true, and does dreaming really set loose the God
trapped inside our souls behind walls of mortality if i could
find out why some peoples dreams never come true, why the
most desperate prayers seem to most often go unanswered,
why the biggest questions cause the most fear, and why my
tears only fall when no ones watching. . .if i could cry, and
free my tears from their prison, i would set them free, i would
set them free, even though they might not change the world if
i could re write history. erase it like a favorite memory lost to
age, and tell the story differently i would. . . but i can't. . . we
are left to read it the way God so permanently wrote it
awaiting the rest of the chapters to find out what in the world
he was thinking i hope you'll be around again, when he
finally writes the ending....'

Skylines

I've lost so many tears inside the empty pockets of drugged out boys.

I've fallen in love with so many cities, and those nights when we weren't infinite, but my god, we were trying.

There were broken hearts littered with alcohol and cigarettes.

We walked down those streets and got so lost we forgot how badly our hearts hurt.

This life was everything, and everything mattered, and everything meant something.

Our *I love yous* were written with backs bent and broken. We were so full, there was nothing empty in our promises.

I lived every day until I felt impossible, and I loved everyone as deeply as they would let me dig.

Ease up off my heavy chest, let me rest through one night without your ghost waking up my silence.

Realize you are worth more than what I would get if I sold all the stars I've ever wished on back to the galaxy.

Forget the journey around the pain, and I will wait. . . to pick up your broken pieces, put your jig sawed heart back together, and then laugh.

Using all the stars we have left.

A Barrage of Rose-Colored Rain

The night after my first one-night stand, I drank an entire pot
of coffee and I showered twice.

I thought about what I had lost, but didn't really miss, and to
this day, the only thing I ever felt guilty of was hiding.

Like pretending his arms didn't feel like home.
I loved so many things about him.

Like the way he touched my back like there were
constellations on my spine. How he walked, naked across the
floor of that studio apartment in NoHo.

My hands quivered like a bassline of tremble.
I never wanted to touch someone so badly.

That night, we were all breaths, all heartbeats, neither of us
said a god damn word. We just laid there.

As gone as our childhoods.
As faded as our fears.
Nobody told us it would feel this way.

That our bodies would cascade into a barrage of rose-colored
rain. That our breathing would crash like an orchestra of
light.

As I watched you sleep, as quiet as a first kiss, I watched your
chest rise and fall. We laughed. We let our hearts go, and all
our fear collapsed, like a fucking lie.

I fell asleep head on your shoulder, with our legs entwined
like the lies we kept telling our fathers.

I don't have all the answers. I just know that when I'm with him, I don't have as many questions.

I don't wonder why or how. I just know how it feels waking up next to him. I know I wanted to keep waking up to his bare chest and his tired eyes.

When I'm with him I know it didn't hurt so bad.
I know, with him, I stopped wanting this life to end.

I know I loved how my face felt in his hands.
How he kept reaching for my arm during that movie.

It was raining.

I know pretending I didn't love that boy almost killed me.

So, if it's still a sin, and heaven really wasn't meant to be a place for men who love other men, I'll stay down here where we don't have to pretend.

I wouldn't want to spend a single moment of my only eternity trapped in a place that couldn't find anything to save, in someone, as beautiful as him.

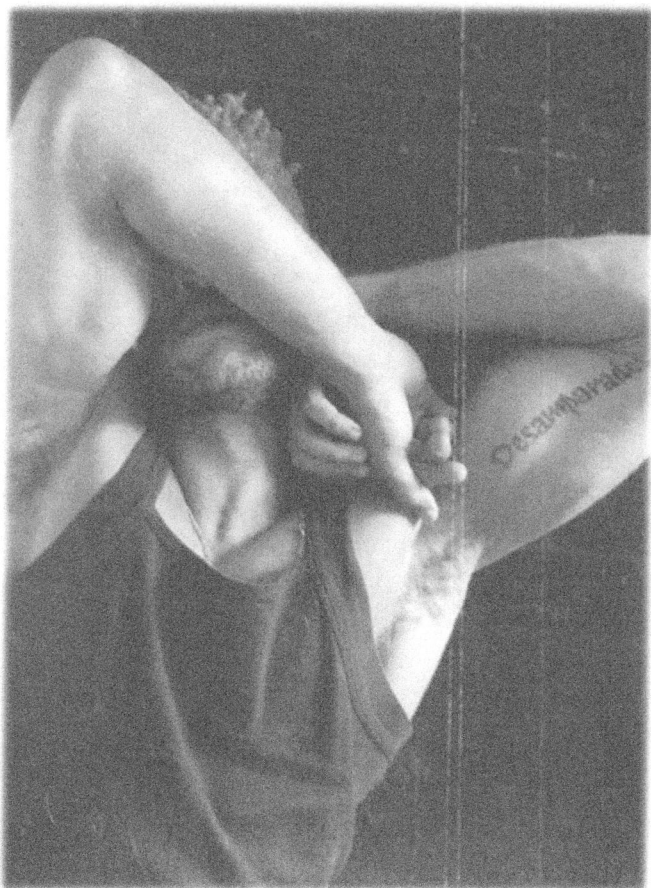

HOW IT ENDS
Part 5

When I'm gone,
Lace my sins with gardenias.
Line my trauma with stars.

gone | lost

To all of those who have loved me from behind the
scenes, I'm so sorry when I'm gone.

I know you miss how easy my lips split open.
How stories would trip over teeth.

How my head flew back, and my laugh sounded like joy
had gotten caught in the back my throat.

It sounded like every love I never let go of.

I'll take the blame for everything.
I know I never made it easy.

I'm so sorry for every lie.

There were entire years where I forgot how to be honest.
I swore and said I was healing.

I know you missed me.
...I did too.

Damion Leigh Morris

One thing I know to be irrevocably true,
Is that if I didn't have you,
there are so many things I'd be so scared to do.

Monster

I stopped being afraid of the dark when I realized…
It's a great place to hide your secrets.

To Whom It May Concern

I guess I never saw this coming.
You never seemed like you were that kind of person.
The kind that up and goes, and never leaves a reason.
Oh, it would have been nice to know who you really were
back then.

What about how we promised to be honest?
I never needed you to be perfect.
We were both to blame, but Babe, I'd have kept on trying.
It would have been nice to know that was never
your intention.

This house is not a home without you in.
I'm doing everything just to forget it.
I drink and smoke, all night alone.
I fuck around this no one town.
Yea, it would have been nice to know
I never mattered to you.

Since we're alone, one last time,
Will you let me say what's on my mind?
You walked away from me, and you
Made it look too easy.

How it Ends

What's gonna happen to all our memories?

No one's loved me like you love me.

If we don't end up together.

Please, remember me forever.

I'll miss the way that you looked at me.

Why does the end feel like a movie?

If we can't stay together,

I swear...

I'll remember you forever.

stay, please

There are days I want to leave.
There are days I don't want to leave, but I want space.
There are days when my love feels buried underneath years
of lonely, and my words feel like ice.

God knows how much you hate the cold.

I couldn't say *I'm sorry* in enough words... or sometimes,
maybe I used too many, but I'm tired of waking up feeling
like I'm hurting you.

If I should leave, I have no idea where I would go.

No clue what I would do.

I can only imagine how many times I would fall apart trying
to fuck you out of my heart. I might fall in love with other
boys, but never as honest. Never as easy. Never as open.

You have too much of me to ever give everything to someone
else, so please keep looking at me the way you did that night
we danced under a festival of lights.

Keep looking at me the way you do every morning before we
crawl out of bed and back into our problems.

Keep looking at me like the night when we laid on the grass
surrounded by thousands of people and billions of lights.

I love how you slow dance with me to my favorite songs,
giving me moments I never thought I would feel in this life.

There are so many nights I can't sleep. There's not a strain
strong enough to smoke me back into my dreams, not a

poem beautiful enough to write me back to bed. So often I stay awake going down the list of all the reasons I could never let you go.

I know you never know how much light is left in my heart.
I know you wake up, and so often it's dark.
I know you feel when my arms don't hold you as tightly, and when my laugh doesn't carry through the home we built.

I know you sometimes have to wait for my eyes to catch yours, the way they do before we crawl out of bed and back into our problems.

I know you know I'll love you more than any other man ever could. I know you know how honest that is.

Loving you was like holding onto a smile and then falling into a bed of big arms. You always made me laugh.
I always made you think.

I loved when you'd write notes in cards even though you thought you could never find the words to say. You always did.

And you didn't walk away. Even though there were so many days when I thought you'd be better off without me. You always stayed.

So, take my hand and let's wrap our arms around the hard times. I will always find a way back to your hands and your chest.

So, stay in this house. Reach for my hand in the darkness. Look me in the eye and tell me all your favorite parts of our story. Please, start at the beginning.

The End

About the Author:

Oh my god! I feel like I've just been talking about myself this whole time. So, like, what do you do?

Contact Me:
Email: blakerwilliams@gmail.com
IG: @thatgreeneyedmixedguy

Made in the USA
Las Vegas, NV
20 November 2021

34927441R00066